CRUCIFIED

Finding through Losing

Studies in the Gospel of Luke

Daily Devotional

Small Group Discussion Guide

Bethany Bible Church

General Editor, Ted Wueste. Additional editing by Ann Kelley, Vickie Grantham,
Michael Donnelly, and Ted Wueste. Design and layout by Courtney Larson.

Introduction, Reflection Questions, Spiritual Practices, and Small Group Studies written by Ted Wueste.
Devotionals written by Joel Nevius, Jim Harte, Ken Morgan, Ted Wueste, Doug Kelley, Michael and Rebekah Stines, and Michael Donnelly.

CONTENTS

CRUCIFIED

INTRODUCTION

What is Crucified?

Crucified is the pattern for living the Christian life. The paradox of life in Christ is that living means dying. Losing means finding. Our natural instinct is to protect and preserve our lives. Jesus did not protect and preserve His life (Luke 22:42). He gave His life so that we might have forgiveness of sin and therefore a grace-based relationship with God. The way that we live this new life is by following the pattern of Christ in taking up our cross daily and dying to self (Luke 9:23). In 1 Corinthians 15, Paul says, "I die daily." The resurrected life is ours in Christ. It has been deposited in our account. We withdraw from that account as we let go of our own resources (death) and take up His (life).

The crucified life is not easy and is often counter-intuitive, but it is worth it! Jesus is not only our Savior but our leader into this life. So, we follow Him.

In these eight weeks, we will be challenged and stretched. We will have the opportunity to put these grand truths into practice as we examine the various ways that we can "lose" in order to find.

Part of our practice will be the spiritual exercise of *prayer and fasting*. Jesus, having taken on human flesh, modeled for us how to live this crucified life through the forty days He spent in the wilderness fasting. He fasted and prayed as He began His ministry. We are encouraged to fast as a part of our life with God as well. Fasting creates space for prayer, stirs our spiritual hunger for God, and reminds us that we are absolutely dependent on God. As we put into practice losing things like food (traditional fasting), we find life in God's presence in deeper ways.

Why Crucified?

In our modern world, we are hungry for more than "cookie cutter" Christianity that is about doing the right things and saying the right things. Life in Christ is about a relationship ... a relationship grounded in prayer and expressed through love ... love for God and others. Our love grows as we grow in letting go of all but Christ. The battle ground is prayer as we follow Jesus into taking up our cross daily.

Our mission as a church is centered on four words: restore, connect, grow, and bless. This study seeks to engage us in all four elements of our mission. We are *restored* as we are shaped into the image of Christ (His pattern of self-sacrificial love; the crucified life). We *connect* as we do life with others (small group element to this study). We *grow* as we deepen our relationship with Jesus (fasting and prayer). We *bless* as we love others the way we have been loved (each small group will be challenged to engage in an outreach project)

How is this Going to Work?

Our eight-week adventure is an "all church experience" and will include every area of our church family, from the youngest child to the oldest adult! The elements of our study will include the following:

1 **Sunday morning sermons** taught by Kent DelHousaye, Brad Pellish, and Ted Wueste. Each week, our pastors will lead us in a study from the Gospel of Luke which describes an aspect of living the crucified life. The challenge will be to explore those invitations from Jesus to let go and take up our cross as we follow Him.

2 **Daily Devotional** (written by the Bethany Bible family). This is what you are holding in your hands. Commit to spend time in reflection and prayer each day as well as a weekly fast of some kind.

3 **Small Group curriculum** (designed to process what God is doing in our lives as we participate in this study). Each person will have an opportunity to join a group for these eight weeks. A group experience is vital because we are grounded in truth in the context of community. There will also be opportunities to reach out as a small group during these eight weeks.

4 **Enrichment Class teaching** (each class will cover materials that go along with the sermons and small groups). Each class will delve deeper into the topic of **fasting**.

5 **Student Ministry and Children's Ministry curriculum**. Make it a priority to discuss and explore what God is doing in your children's lives. If you don't have a child or a child at home, pray for our families who are journeying together!

6 **Worship CD** with original songs (written by the BBC worship ministry) that complement the themes for each week. Use this CD in your daily times of prayer and reflection and ask God to deepen your heart for Him.

The challenge for our church body is to **commit to four things**:

1 Attend the weekly worship service and our study of the Gospel of Luke. If you can't make it on a Sunday morning, you can listen online or request an audio recording.

2 Read the daily devotional. The commitment is six days per week for about 20 minutes each day. Of course, you can go as far and deep with this study as you desire.

3 Participate in a weekly fast of some kind. (see the information on fasting that follows)

4 Participate in a weekly small group experience. We'll get you connected and help facilitate the process.

How to Use this Devotional Guide
Each week, this devotional guide offers several encouragements. Day 1 is a reflection and time of prayer concerning the weekly fast. Days 2, 4, and 5 are devotional readings that reflect on the weekly theme related to Crucified. On Day 3, you'll find reflection questions designed to help you process your response to God and what He might be doing in you. Finally, Day 6 is a journal to think through and reflect on your week.

Use the devotional guide as a place to take notes and prayerfully interact with God. Let Him lead you and trust Him to deepen your desire for Him.

Community Group Discussion
At the end of each week's devotional readings and exercises, you'll find a discussion guide for small group interaction. Use this during your weekly time in discussion. The only preparation necessary is to have listened to the sermon and reflected on the daily devotionals.

What is Fasting?
"A fast is the self-denial of normal necessities in order to intentionally attend to God in prayer. Bringing attachments and cravings to the surface opens a place for prayer. This physical awareness of emptiness is the reminder to turn to Jesus who alone can satisfy."

Adele Calhoun, *Spiritual Disciplines Handbook*

The Purpose of Fasting
The purpose of fasting is to stir our hunger for God. It is not bad things that draw us away as much as the "desire for other things." (Mark 4:19)

Meanwhile the disciples were urging him, saying, "Rabbi, eat." But he said to them, "I have food to eat that you do not know about." So the disciples said to one another, "Has anyone brought him something to eat?" Jesus said to them, "My food is to do the will of him who sent me and to accomplish his work." (John 4:31-34)

Fasting reminds us that our true food is our life with God.

John Piper wrote that "the discipline of self-denial is fraught with dangers – perhaps only surpassed by the dangers of indulgence." Fasting is a tool that we utilize to deepen our prayer life. It is a means, not an end.

Fasting Basics and FAQs

Our challenge to a weekly fast of some kind will include various things. However, if you choose to do a fast from food, here are a few guidelines to keep in mind.

- Don't fast when you are sick, traveling, pregnant or nursing. People with diabetes, gout, liver disease, kidney disease, ulcers, hypoglycemia, cancer and blood diseases should not fast.
- Don't fast if you are in a hurry and are fasting for immediate results regarding some decision. Fasting is not magic.
- Listen for a nudging from God to fast. Let Him set the agenda.
- Stay hydrated. Always drink plenty of water and fluids.
- If you are new to fasting, begin by fasting for one meal. Spend the time with God that you would normally be eating.
- Work up to longer fasts. Don't attempt prolonged fasts without guidance. Check with your doctor before attempting long periods of fasting.
- If you decide to fast regularly, give your body time to adjust to new rhythms of eating. You may feel more tired on days you fast. Adjust your responsibilities appropriately. (Expect your tongue to feel coated, and expect to have bad breath.)
- Begin a fast after supper. Fast until supper the next day. This way you miss two, rather than three, meals.
- Don't break your fast with a huge meal. Eat small portions of food.

CRUCIFIED

WEEK 1 | FINDING LIFE

And he said to all, "If anyone would come after me, let him deny himself and take up his cross daily and follow me. For whoever would save his life will lose it, but whoever loses his life for my sake will save it. For what does it profit a man if he gains the whole world and loses or forfeits himself? For whoever is ashamed of me and of my words, of him will the Son of Man be ashamed when he comes in his glory and the glory of the Father and of the holy angels. But I tell you truly, there are some standing here who will not taste death until they see the kingdom of God."

Luke 9:23-27

Sermon Notes | Luke 9:23-27

Day 1 – Prayer and Fasting

Weekly Fasting Challenge: *examine and understand fasting*

Consider the following passage:

> "And when you fast, do not look gloomy like the hypocrites, for they disfigure their faces that their fasting may be seen by others. Truly, I say to you, they have received their reward. But when you fast, anoint your head and wash your face that your fasting may not be seen by others but by your Father who is in secret. And your Father who sees in secret will reward you." Matthew 6:16-18

> *"Almost everywhere at all times, fasting has held a place of great importance since it is closely linked with the intimate sense of religion. Perhaps this is the explanation for the demise of fasting in our day. When the sense of God diminishes, fasting disappears."*

> *Edward Farrell, quoted in* A Hunger for God, *by John Piper, Crossway Books, 1997.*

Prayer: Talk to God about how you feel about fasting. Ask Him to shape your approach that it might honor Him.

Plan: What will your fast be this week? Choose something simple: a meal, a day with no television, or perhaps fasting from some other regular activity.

What will you do?

When will you do it?

Scripture for Prayer/Meditation during fasting:
Luke 9:23-25

Day 2 – A Voice from our Christian Heritage

You have one precious life: *Is TV too big a part of it?*
John Piper

If all other variables are equal, your capacity to know God deeply will probably diminish in direct proportion to how much television you watch. There are several reasons for this. One is that television reflects American culture at its most trivial. And a steady diet of triviality shrinks the soul. You get used to it. It starts to seem normal. Silly becomes funny. And funny becomes pleasing. And pleasing becomes soul-satisfaction. And in the end the soul that is made for God has shrunk to fit snugly around triteness.

This may be unnoticed, because if all you've known is American culture, you can't tell there is anything wrong. If you have only read comic books, it won't be strange that there are no novels in your house. If you live where there are no seasons, you won't miss the colors of fall. If you watch fifty TV ads each night, you may forget there is such a thing as wisdom. TV is mostly trivial. It seldom inspires great thoughts or great feelings with glimpses of great Truth. God is great, absolute, all-shaping Reality. If He gets any air time, He is treated as an opinion. There is no reverence. No trembling. God and all that He thinks about the world is missing. Cut loose from God, everything goes down.

Just think how new TV is. In the 2000 years since Christ, TV has shaped only the last 2.5 percent of that history. For 97.5 percent of the time since Jesus, there was no TV. And for 95 percent of this time there was no radio. It arrived on the scene in the early 1900's. So for 1900 years of Christian history, people spent their leisure time doing other things. We wonder, what could they possibly have done? They may have read more. Or discussed things more. For certain they were not bombarded with soul-shrinking, round-the-clock trivialities.

Do you ever ask, "What could I accomplish that is truly worthwhile if I did not watch TV?" You see, it isn't just what TV does to us with its rivers of emptiness; it is also what TV keeps us from doing. Why not try something? Make a list of what you might accomplish if you took the time you spend watching TV and devoted it to something else. For example:

- You might be inspired to some great venture by learning about the life of a noble saint like Amy Carmichael and how she found courage to go alone to serve the children of India. Where do such radical dreams come from? Not from watching TV. Open your soul to be blown away by some unspeakable life of dedication to a great cause.
- You might be inspired by a biography of a businessman or doctor or nurse to work hard for the skills to bless others with the excellence of your profession devoted to a higher end than anything you will see commended on TV, which never includes Jesus Christ.
- You might memorize the eight chapters of Paul's letter to the Romans, and penetrate to the depths of his vision of God, and discover the precious power of memorized scripture in your life and ministry to others. No one could estimate the power that would come to a church if we all turned the TV off for one month and devoted that same amount of time to memorizing scripture.
- You might write a simple poem or a letter to a parent or a child or friend or a colleague expressing deep gratitude for their life or a longing for their soul.
- You might make a cake or a casserole for new neighbors and take it to them with a smile and an invitation to visit some time and get to know each other.

So there are good reasons to try a TV fast. Or to simply wean yourself off of it entirely. We have not owned a TV for thirty-four years of marriage except for three years in Germany when we used it for language learning. There is no inherent virtue in this. I only mention it to prove that you can raise five culturally sensitive and

Biblically informed children without it. They never complained about it. In fact they often wondered out loud how people found the time to watch as much as they do.

Day 3 – Reflection Questions

What new insights do you have about Luke 9:23-27?

What do you believe God is personally saying to you from these verses?

How are you seeing God at work in you so far this week?

Do you have any fears related to "taking up your cross" and "losing your life"?

How will "losing your life" look in your life? Ponder a few ways ...

Day 4 – A Voice from Bethany

Finding Life...By Letting Go
Luke 9:23-27
Joel Nevius

Recently, my wife and I bought a house. For those of us who don't have a lot of money, it also means that we had to let go of our old house. We couldn't keep it. We had to let go of the attachments we had with it because of the time we spent renovating it and the fond memories we created there.

Jesus, in Luke 9:23, offers an invitation for anyone to find life with him, but he gives it under a condition: "let him deny himself." The word for 'deny' really means to contradict. He's saying, "If anyone wants to follow me and find life in me, then you have to contradict yourself."

There is a basic law of logic called, "the law of non-contradiction." It means that for any proposition, it cannot be both truth and false at the same time and in the same way.

For instance, I cannot live in my old house and in my new house at the same time and in the same way. Here, Jesus is giving us two exclusive possibilities: we either live for him or we live for ourselves. It's a logical contradiction to say that we live for him, and at the same time live for ourselves. To "deny" ourselves is to take a step to contradict our old way of living. To deny that I am living at my old house, I have to take a step. I have to move out.

To follow Jesus, we need to pack up and move out of ourselves.

In the very next verse (24), Jesus takes this idea further and equates denying oneself with losing his/her "life." In order to find life in and with Jesus, we have to be willing to lose what we think brings life: our desire for autonomous control; our sinful appetite to arrange life the way we think is best; our need to be "free" from supposed constraints that would take away the right to our own happiness.

Jesus wants to offer us a new home in himself. But we have to be willing to let go and contradict the fallen inclinations of our souls. This is the secret to finding true life.

In this passage, Jesus is being logical, yet paradoxical. We cannot keep ourselves if we want to keep Christ. Once we forfeit, we'll win. Once we die, we'll live. Once we surrender, we'll be victorious.

It's a contradiction to live for Christ and to live for us. What are you willing to let go of: Christ, or yourself? Jesus says that we can't hold on to both.

Jesus, I don't even know what to begin letting go of. I want to follow you, because living for myself is causing me to lose myself. Through your Holy Spirit, reveal one thing to me this week to lose, because I want to be found in you. Amen.

Day 5 – A Voice from Bethany

Not My Will, But …
Luke 9:23-27
Ted Wueste

Jesus never asks us to go somewhere that He hasn't gone. This is part of the beauty of the incarnation. God the Son took on human flesh and took up His cross. His whole life was one, long walk to the cross. He could have avoided it, He could have run, but He believed that there was something better than self-preservation and self-promotion.

In those last hours before His death, He prayed fervently:

> "Father, if you are willing, remove this cup from me.
> Nevertheless, not my will, but yours, be done." (Luke 22:42)

Jesus modeled so many things in this simple prayer. He modeled honesty: for those who are wrapped in human flesh, there are struggle and choices. Honesty is needed or the struggle goes undercover and becomes more powerful. Second, He modeled surrender. He surrendered Himself when He had the power to take matters into His own hands. He could have removed the cup on His own. Third, He modeled the need for prayer even when we know the outcome of a matter. Jesus knew what was coming and desired deeply what the cross would accomplish. He prayed because life is not about gritting our teeth and enduring, but doing life with God. Finally, He modeled the specifics of our struggle: will it be my will or His will that prevails?

In Philippians 2:5-7, the Apostle Paul gives us a picture of this crucified life:

> "Have this mind among yourselves, which is yours in Christ
> Jesus, who, though he was in the form of God, did not count

equality with God a thing to be grasped, but made himself nothing, taking the form of a servant, being born in the likeness of men."

The core perspective that Jesus held was that His equality with God (His very deity) was not something to be grasped (the Greek word is "used to one's advantage"). If we are to take up our cross and follow, we are challenged to not look at anything in our lives (strengths, resources, talents, gifts) as being about us. They are about God and His good purposes.

To say "not my will, but yours, be done" requires that we know who we are and what our will is. It also requires meditating on His goodness and perfection. How well do you know yourself? How well do you know Him and His purposes?

PRAYER: Father, show me my heart. Show me those places where my will conflicts with You. Father, You are perfect and good and loving. I choose You above all other things. Amen

Day 6 – Journal

How did you see God at work in you this week?

What did you notice about your "life with God" this week?

What was encouraging?

What was challenging?

How is your desire for Him shifting this week?

What was it like to fast this week?

Small Group Discussion for Week 1 ... Finding Life

Prayer/Reflection
Begin with a few moments of quiet before the Lord

Group leader: read through Luke 9:23-27 quietly as group members listen prayerfully.
After the reading, allow for 1-2 minutes of silence to notice what stands out to your heart from the passage.

Is there anyone in the group that would like to share what stood out to them?

Review
What was the main idea of the teaching this week?

What are the implications?

*Why does it matter in your life? (be specific to your life, not people in general)
(allow time/space for all in the group to share)*

Practice
From what did you fast? (use caution - consider Matthew 6:16-18)

How was your experience of the fast?

What have you seen God doing in you through this fast?

Share
*What else have you noticed about your life with God in the past days/week?
(look back at your journal)*

Prayer
How can the group pray for your growth in this part of living a Crucified life?

(pray for one another)

WEEK 2 | LOSING AMBITION

An argument arose among them as to which of them was the greatest. But Jesus, knowing the reasoning of their hearts, took a child and put him by his side and said to them, "Whoever receives this child in my name receives me, and whoever receives me receives him who sent me. For he who is least among you all is the one who is great."

Luke 9:46-48

Sermon Notes | Luke 9:46-48

Day 1 – Prayer and Fasting

Weekly Fasting Challenge: *repentance and grief*

Consider the following passage:

And when Ahab heard those words, he tore his clothes and put sackcloth on his flesh and fasted and lay in sackcloth and went about dejectedly. And the word of the LORD came to Elijah the Tishbite, saying, "Have you seen how Ahab has humbled himself before me?"   1 Kings 21:27-29

"Holy and lawful fasting has three objectives. We use it either to weaken and subdue the flesh that it may not act wantonly, or that we may be better prepared for prayers and holy meditations, or that it may be a testimony of our self-abasement before God when we wish to confess our guilt before him."
        John Calvin, Institutes of the Christian Religion, Vol. 2, p. 1241 (IV, xii, 15).

Prayer: Pray Psalm 139:23-24. Read through the verses. Meditate on them. Put the verses in your own words and pray them back to God.

Plan: Fast from *food* for some time period this week. Use the time you would normally eat for repentance and to ask the Lord to search your heart. *Note:* see the guidelines for fasting in the introduction. If you don't choose food, choose some other normal activity.

What will you do?

When will you do it?

Scripture for Prayer/Meditation during fasting:
Psalm 139:23-24

Day 2 – A Voice from our Christian Heritage

The Importance of Self-Judgment
A.W.Tozer

Hardly anything else reveals so well the fear and uncertainty among men as the length to which they will go to hide their true selves from each other and even from their own eyes.

Almost all men live from childhood to death behind a semi opaque curtain, coming out briefly only when forced by some emotional shock and then retreating as quickly as possible into hiding again. The result of this lifelong dissimulation is that people rarely know their neighbors for what they really are, and worse than that, the camouflage is so successful that they do not know themselves either.

Self-knowledge is so critically important to us in our pursuit of God and His righteousness that we lie under heavy obligation to do immediately whatever is necessary to remove the disguise and permit our real selves to be known. It is one of the supreme tragedies in religion that so many of us thinks so highly of ourselves when the evidence lies all on the other side; and our self-admiration effectively blocks out any possible effort to discover a remedy for our condition. Only the man who knows he is sick will go to a physician.

Now, our true moral and spiritual state can be disclosed only by the Spirit and the Word. The final judgment of the heart is God's. There is a sense in which we dare not judge each other (Matt. 7:1-5), and in which we should not even try to judge ourselves (1 Cor. 4:3) The ultimate judgment belongs to the One whose eyes are like a flame of fire and who sees quite through the deeds and thoughts of men. I am glad to leave the final word to Him.

There is, nevertheless, a place for self-judgment and a real need that we exercise it (1 Cor. 11:31, 32). While our self-discovery is not likely to be complete and our self-judgment is almost certain to be biased and imperfect, there is yet every good reason for us to work along with the Holy Spirit in His benign effort to locate us spiritually in order that we may make such amendments as the circumstances demand. That God already knows us thoroughly is certain (Ps. 139:1-6) It remains for us to know ourselves as accurately as possible. For this reason I offer some rules for self-discovery; and if the results are not all we could desire they may be at least better than not at all. We may be known by the following:

1. *What we want most.* We have but to get quiet, recollect our thoughts, wait for the mild excitement within us to subside, and then listen closely for the faint cry of desire. Ask your heart: what would you rather have than anything else in the world? Reject the conventional answer. Insist on the true one...

2. *What we think about most.* The necessities of life compel us to think about many things, but the true test is what we think about voluntarily. It is more than likely that our thoughts cluster about our secret heart treasure, and whatever that is will reveal what we are. "Where your treasure is, there will your heart be also."

3. *How we use our money.* Again we must ignore those matters about which we are not altogether free. We must pay taxes and provide the necessities of life for ourselves and family, if any. That is routine, merely, and tells us little about ourselves. But whatever money is left to do with as we please - that will tell us a great deal indeed.

4. *What we do with our leisure time.* A large share of our time is already spoken for by the exigencies of civilized living, but we do have some free time. What we do with it is vital. Most people waste it staring at the television, listening to the radio, reading the cheap output of the press or engaging in idle chatter. What I do with mine reveals the kind of man I am.

5. *The company we enjoy.* There is a law of moral attraction that draws every man to the society most like himself. "Being let go, they went to their own company." Where we go when we are free to go where we will is a near-infallible index of character.

6. *Whom and what we desire.* I have long suspected that the great majority of evangelical Christians, while kept somewhat in line by the pressure of group opinion, nevertheless have a boundless, if perforce secret, admiration for the world. We can learn the true state of our minds by examining our unexpressed admirations. Israel often admired, even envied, the pagan nations around them, and so forgot the adoption and the glory and the covenants and the law and the promise and the fathers. Instead of blaming Israel let us look to ourselves.

7. *What we laugh at.* No one with due regard for the wisdom of God would argue that there is anything wrong with laughter, since humor is a legitimate component of our complex nature. Lacking a sense of humor we fall that much short of healthy humanity.

There are a few tests. The wise Christian will find others.

Day 3 – Reflection Questions

What new insights do you have about Luke 9:46-48?

What do you believe God is personally saying to you from these verses?

How are you seeing God at work in you so far this week?

How have you seen ambition rear its ugly head in your life?

How will "losing ambition" look in your life? Ponder a few ways...

Day 4 – A Voice from Bethany

Becoming the Least
Luke 9:46-48
Rene Fillingame

Luke 9:46-48, Matthew 18:1-5, and Mark 9:33-37 all recount the same story with slight variations. Take several minutes to read through these scriptures.

In context, Jesus had recently healed a demon-possessed boy and the crowds were marveling at God's greatness. As Jesus and His disciples began their journey to Capernaum, He reminded them that He would suffer, be betrayed, and killed. Naturally, as the disciples ponder this statement, they begin to discuss "If Jesus goes, who will take over, be the leader? Who is the greatest among us twelve?"

Arriving at their destination, Jesus asked the disciples what they were discussing on the road. Of course, He already knew but wanted them to admit it. Silence. Crickets. Jesus knew what they needed and it was something my mom used to call "a piece of humble pie". Luke 9:47, 48 states that Jesus drew a child to Himself saying, "Whoever receives this child in My name receives Me, and whoever receives Me receives Him who sent Me; for the one who is least among all of you, this is the one who is great."

I love the way Eugene Peterson's *The Message* puts it: "You become great by accepting, not asserting."

Jesus modeled greatness this way—by accepting/receiving God's will, by becoming the least. He left His heavenly home to be born as a baby, to serve the poor, the sick, the outcast, and ultimately to offer His life as the sacrifice for sin.

So how do we "become the least"? I believe the answer to that question is in the word "receiving", which is repeated four times in verse 48. We begin to become the least when we humbly receive Christ as Savior. And then we continue to become the least as we humbly receive/accept the circumstances God has orchestrated for us and receiving the people He has placed in our lives.

Several years ago, God asked me to become the least with a very close relative. She wrongfully accused me of being unkind and mean and everything within me wanted to defend myself. Instead, only by the power of His Holy Spirit within, was I able to humbly listen and love her during this time.

What or who has God asked you to receive and accept today? Open up and take a bite of humble pie, and in so doing, you are on the path to true greatness by becoming the least.

Day 5 – A Voice from Bethany

Born Again, and Again, and Again….
Jim Harte

Listen to a four-year-old boy pray one night in the presence of his father. "Jesus, thank you for dying to take away my sins, and thank you that you give them back." This child is obviously not ashamed of his thoughts about God. He takes joy in being who he is. This innocence naturally trusts in another. This child feels safe in the presence of his father. He trusts his father. It is a safe place.

Our fallen, sin-shaped world devours this innocence. And this world has shaped my heart. How do I know?

Once, over our morning coffee, I asked, "Jo Ann, what is the image you believe I am trying to communicate to others with my life?" Her first few answers were a little fluffy: "spiritual, generous, and loving." After about thirty minutes of quiet, she looked up from the book she was reading, "Competent."

That was it! Competence. She was right. It was one of the images. The desire to be the greatest is always present with me; to be the hero of the stories running through my mind. The need to project this image has meant that it has not felt safe to be who I truly am. My sin-shaped heart shouts, "Jim, you have to prove yourself in order to be acceptable!" Who can I trust with the reality of who I am? No one, not even myself.

Jesus says, "Jim, I know about the reasoning of your heart." He knows I am hiding, dressed in the image of competence. He knows I am terrified. Jesus is telling me, "Jim, if you want the rewards of feeling acceptable and safe in OUR love, you must submit to the mortifying ordeal of being human."

Listen again (read it out loud) to the prayer of our four-year-old. Is this how you and I pray, unashamed of our thoughts? What is it about a child? I can never remember a time when, concerned about my appearance, I did not need to cover myself up. How can I recapture the joy of being a child?

Our child is like Jesus. The joy of being a child is in serving as a child. I am drawn into the heart of God – to listen and watch and learn what it means to be a child again, shaped by His person and gifts. It is safe here. Jesus offers himself and the Father as a gift. What child does not like gifts?

Competence has a problem with gifts. They must be earned.

Against the almost irresistible tug of the world, I am learning to trust Him with the reasoning of my heart. Jesus is telling the truth about what it means to be a child: taking joy in who I am. Very slowly, I am growing into embracing this.

Jesus makes this a matter of death into life.

Childlikeness is a miracle. Born again, and again, and again.

Day 6 – Journal

How did you see God at work in you this week?

What did you notice about your "life with God" this week?

What was encouraging?

What was challenging?

How is your desire for Him shifting this week?

What was it like to fast this week?

Small Group Discussion for Week 2 ... Losing Ambition

Prayer/Reflection
Begin with a few moments of quiet before the Lord

Group leader: read through Luke 9:46-48 quietly as group members imagine that they are in the scene described. After the reading, allow for 1 minute of silence ... encourage group members to quietly reflect on what it is like to be received as a child. Read through the passage one more time, followed by a prayer for the group.

What came to your heart and mind as you considered being received as a child?

How does this impact the way you interact with God? Others? Life itself?

Review
What was the main idea of the teaching this week?

What are the implications?

*Why does it matter in your life? (be specific to your life, not people in general)
    (allow time/space for all in the group to share)*

Practice
From what did you fast? (use caution - consider Matthew 6:16-18)

How has your experience of the fast been?

What have you seen God doing in you through this fast?

Share
*What else have you noticed about your life with God in the past days/week?
    (look back at your journal from the previous weeks)*

Prayer

How can the group pray for your growth in this part of living a Crucified life?

(pray for one another)

WEEK 3 | LOSING ATTACHMENTS

As they were going along the road, someone said to him, "I will follow you wherever you go." And Jesus said to him, "Foxes have holes, and birds of the air have nests, but the Son of Man has nowhere to lay his head." To another he said, "Follow me." But he said, "Lord, let me first go and bury my father." And Jesus said to him, "Leave the dead to bury their own dead. But as for you, go and proclaim the kingdom of God." Yet another said, "I will follow you, Lord, but let me first say farewell to those at my home." Jesus said to him, "No one who puts his hand to the plow and looks back is fit for the kingdom of God."

Luke 9:57-62

Sermon Notes | Luke 9:57-62

Day 1 – Prayer and Fasting

Weekly Fasting Challenge: *discernment/decisions*

Consider the following passage:

"I wept and humbled my soul with fasting ..." Psalm 69:10

"Of fasting I say this: it is right to fast frequently in order to subdue and control the body. For when the stomach is full, the body does not serve for preaching, for praying, for studying, or for doing anything else that is good. Under such circumstances God's word cannot remain. But one should not fast with a view to meriting something by it as by a good work." Martin Luther, *What Luther Says*, Vol. 1, compiled by Ewald M. Plass, p. 506

Prayer: Take the words of Psalm 69:1-3 and apply them to your life. Pray them based on a decision or challenge you are facing.

Plan: Are you facing a crisis ... a decision? Is someone else in your life in need of guidance? Make a plan to fast from "analysis" and problem solving so that you can pray and listen to God.

What might this look like for you?

Scripture for Prayer/Meditation during fasting:
Psalm 27:14

Day 2 – A Voice from our Christian Heritage

A Savior from Sin, Not from Pain
Larry Crabb

The dragon can look like a dove. He can encourage us to hate adult movies and abortion and rape, to never miss church, and to be there for hurting friends, when all the while our commitment to a better life, however we define it, occupies first place in our hearts. The only consistent message coming from the world, the flesh, and the devil is this: *Seek your deepest enjoyment somewhere else than in God.*

Jesus came to earth to tell us He is the way, the truth and the life. His death opened the *way* into God's presence, the greatest blessing of all. His teaching made clear the *truth* that life does not consist in a return to Eden's comforts; it doesn't even consist in graduation to heaven's bliss. True life is knowing God. Jesus said so. And the *life* is Christ himself, not the bread He could multiply or the corpse He could resurrect, but Him. Being in Him, having Him in us, living with His energy, chasing after His purpose, loving what He loves, seeing Him form in us until we're actually like Him – that's life. And it can be enjoyed in bankruptcy or affluence, from a hospital bed or a deck chair on a cruise ship, or when you walk out of a divorce court you never thought you'd see or into a surprise party celebrating fifty years of your wonderful marriage.

When we live the Old Way, we don't believe what Jesus said. Anne Graham Lotz isn't making that mistake. I listened to her on a tape where she recounted some hardships in her life, then said, "Don't give me sympathy. Don't give me advice. Don't give me a miracle. *Just give me Jesus!*"

The Old Way sees things differently. The dragon thoughtfully suggests, "Yes, you do want Jesus. He's the one who can restore your marriage, provide great ideas on raising kids that really work, and prosper your ministry. Jesus teaches principles to live by, He offers methods to follow that will give you the life you want. What must you do to be saved from persecution and trouble? He'll tell you. Go to Him to find out what you must do to make life work!

I'm learning to distinguish between the dragon's voice and the spirit's. The dragon directs my attention from the person of Christ as the source of the deepest joy toward the blessings of life as what I really need to be happy. If those blessings can be gained only by obvious sin, fine; if living a good Christian life keeps life working well, that's fine too. The dragon doesn't care, as long as I chase after the Better Life of Blessings. After listening to the three-headed dragon for a while, I tend to see Christ as savior from pain, not from sin; as a responsive benefactor rather than Holy Lord.

The spirit always points to the Christ of the Bible, the One who offers no guarantees that my marriage will survive, that the biopsy will yield good news, or that I won't lose my job. The spirit exposes a problem in my soul worse than my suffering, then reveals the God of grace. He tells me I can know this God; I can know His heart, rest in His power, and hope in His purposes. And I can see it all in Christ. He keeps stirring my heart to say, "Just give me Jesus!"

Day 3 – Reflection Questions

What new insights do you have about Luke 9:57-62?

What do you believe God is personally saying to you from these verses?

How are you seeing God at work in you so far this week?

What "attachments" do you need to lose?

Day 4 – A Voice from Bethany

Losing Attachments
Luke 9: 57-62
Michael Donnelly

Webster's New World Dictionary: Detach.
  1. to separate especially from a larger mass and usually without violence or damage.
  2. to disengage or withdraw.

At the end of Luke 9, we are given a small glimpse of three men who wished to join Jesus as He set out to walk the road for His Journey to Jerusalem. We are told twice in preceding verses that Jesus "set His face" before beginning His journey to Jerusalem. With my mind's eye, I try to imagine His physical presence and earnestly meditate to understand the gaze our Lord may have had as He speaks to each of these three men. For me it is significant that Luke provides three individual occurrences of Jesus' encounters, making clear that following Him requires my focus to change.

Each of these three men represents an attachment to a level of personal security that I possess. I rest for a moment in the verses and with prayerful reflection look to see "His face set" towards Jerusalem. I imagine for a brief moment His eyes coming to rest on my anxious gaze; He holds the depth of the universe in that gaze. I hear Him ask, "Will you be willing to accept homelessness and hunger?" Or, as He asked the second man, "If burying the dead is your reason to hesitate today, what reason will you hold tomorrow?" Or, to the third man - my third fear - He asks, "Is who or what you are leaving behind more important than Who you are following?" I feel a lump in my throat.

The Scripture is merciful; it does not tell us how these men decide. Rather, I am left to notice the common thread between these three men and myself.

A personal decision is necessary and no one else can decide for me. As I lean into my faith, which attachments hold me in tension creating this palpable resistance between my relationship with the

Lord and my relationships with security, ceremony and sentimentality? Daily I ask for His strength to "set my face" towards His path and for the courage to lean further into my relationship with my Savior.

Day 5 – A Voice from Bethany

Faith is an Empty Hand
Luke 9:57-62
Ted Wueste

We have a natural tendency to cling tightly to things when we are fearful. We cling to the bar of the rollercoaster. We cling to whatever we can when riding in the car with our teenager who is learning to drive! Spiritually, we cling to various things when we're afraid as well … it might be the seeming security of money or perhaps the love and esteem of others. It's possible that we cling to almost anything that we believe can make things okay.

When Jesus calls us to follow, there is fear. It's normal. We are fearful because we are moving into unknown territory. To have no fear is to deny reality. This is the very reason that "do not fear" is the most common command in the Bible. Following Jesus means that we are challenged to "lose" and it can be scary to lose things, especially things that have brought us comfort or joy or security. The good news is that what we gain is far more satisfying and good and perfect than what we lose, but we already know that. It's prying our hands off the old things that can be so difficult.

There is an old story of hunters in Africa who would hunt monkeys for food. Their tactic was simple and based on something they knew about the nature of monkeys. They would take a coconut, hollow it out, and place a sweet treat inside. Monkeys would come along and smell the treat and stick their hand inside the hole. The hole was just big enough to allow the hand to go in and too small for the monkey to withdraw his hand filled with the treat. So, not wanting to let go of the food, the monkey would get stuck. The hunters approach while the monkey desperately tries to remove its hand with the treat. Though knowing that harm is sure to come, the monkey refuses to release what it believes will satisfy its desires.

We can often be the same. We get stuck. We get caught up in things that we know will harm us, but letting go is not easy.

It takes faith to let go. Faith is difficult when we believe that things other than Jesus can truly satisfy us. The reality is that clinging to anything but Jesus is always a trap – it will always lead to imprisonment and to living in ways that are less than our design.

Faith is an unclenched hand. But the hand only unclenches when there is trust in something better. Put into your own words what that something better is ...

PRAYER: Father, give me eyes to see your glory, to see that you are better and more satisfying than any created thing. Father, give me strength to let go of those things which get me stuck. Father, thank you for loving me right where I am, and for loving me too much to leave me there. Amen.

Day 6 – Journal

How did you see God at work in you this week?

What did you notice about your "life with God" this week?

What was encouraging?

What was challenging?

How is your desire for Him shifting this week?

What was it like to fast this week?

Small Group Discussion for Week 3 ... Losing Attachments

Prayer/Reflection
Begin with a time of praying together ... praising God for what He is doing in your lives! Offer simple, sentence prayers praising Him and thanking Him.

Group participant: read Luke 9:57-62.

Group members listen attentively as the passage is read a second time.

Reflect: *If you were one of the characters in the account, which one would you be? Why?*

   Share with the group.

Review
What was the main idea of the teaching this week?

What are the implications?

Why does it matter in your life? (be specific to your life, not people in general)
   (allow time/space for all in the group to share)

Practice
From what did you fast? (use caution - consider Matthew 6:16-18)

How has your experience of the fast been?

What have you seen God doing in you through this fast?

Share
What else have you noticed about your life with God in the past days/week?
   (look back at your journal from the previous weeks)

Prayer
How can the group pray for your growth in this part of living a Crucified life?

(pray for one another)

WEEK 4 | LOSING ANXIETY

Now as they went on their way, Jesus entered a village. And a woman
named Martha welcomed him into her house. And she had a sister
called Mary, who sat at the Lord's feet and listened to his teaching.
But Martha was distracted with much serving. And she went up to
him and said, "Lord, do you not care that my sister has left me to
serve alone? Tell her then to help me." But the Lord answered
her, "Martha, Martha, you are anxious and troubled about many
things, but one thing is necessary. Mary has chosen the good portion,
which will not be taken away from her."

Luke 10:38-42

Sermon Notes | Luke 10:38-42; 12:22-31

Day 1 – Prayer and Fasting

Weekly Fasting Challenge: *deeper relationship with God*

Consider the following passage:

"For God alone my soul waits in silence; from him comes my salvation. He only is my rock and my salvation, my fortress; I shall not be greatly shaken." Psalm 62:1-2

"Fasting is a help to prayer; particularly when we set apart larger portions of time for private prayer. Then especially it is that God is often pleased to lift the souls of his servants above all the things of earth, and sometimes to wrap them up, as it were, into the third heaven. And it is chiefly, as it is an help to prayer, that it has so frequently been found a means, in the hands of God, of confirming and increasing, not one virtue, not chastity only (as some have idly imagined, without any ground from Scripture, reason, or experience) but also seriousness of spirit, earnestness, sensibility, and tenderness of conscious, deadness to the world, and consequently the love of God, and every heavenly and holy affection." John Wesley, "Sermon XXVII, On Our Lord's Sermon on the Mount," *The Works of John Wesley, Vol. 5,* p. 441.

Prayer: Pray through Psalm 62:1-2. Ask the Lord about some activity which you can "silence" in order to focus on Him.

Plan: Choose some normal activity like watching TV, listening to the radio in the car, or social media. Take one day and fast from that activity.

What will you do?

When will you do it?

Scripture for Prayer/Meditation during fasting:
Luke 12:31

Day 2 – A Voice from our Christian Heritage

One of God's Great "Don'ts"
Oswald Chambers

Do not fret— it only causes harm —Psalm 37:8

Fretting means getting ourselves "out of joint" mentally or spiritually. It is one thing to say, "Do not fret," but something very different to have such a nature that you find yourself unable to fret. It's easy to say, "Rest in the Lord, and wait patiently for Him" (Psalm 37:7) until our own little world is turned upside down and we are forced to live in confusion and agony like so many other people. Is it possible to "rest in the Lord" then? If this "Do not" doesn't work there, then it will not work anywhere. This "Do not" must work during our days of difficulty and uncertainty, as well as our peaceful days, or it will never work. And if it will not work in your particular case, it will not work for anyone else. Resting in the Lord is not dependent on your external circumstances at all, but on your relationship with God Himself.

Worrying always results in sin. We tend to think that a little anxiety and worry are simply an indication of how wise we really are, yet it is actually a much better indication of just how wicked we are. Fretting rises from our determination to have our own way. Our Lord never worried and was never anxious, because His purpose was never to accomplish His own plans but to fulfill God's plans. Fretting is wickedness for a child of God.

Have you been propping up that foolish soul of yours with the idea that your circumstances are too much for God to handle? Set all your opinions and speculations aside and "abide under the shadow of the Almighty" (Psalm 91:1). Deliberately tell God that you will not fret about whatever concerns you. All our fretting and worrying is caused by planning without God.

Day 3 – Reflection Questions

What new insights do you have about Luke 10:38-42?

What stood out to you from Luke 12:22-31?

What do you believe God is personally saying to you from these verses?

How are you seeing God at work in you so far this week?

What anxieties are present in your life? What might it look like to entrust them to God's care? Is there an underlying expectation that you need to release?

Day 4 – A Voice from Bethany

Only One Thing Is Necessary
(and it's not anxiety)
Doug Kelley

Tomorrow morning I'm meeting with a friend who wants to talk about the effect that anxiety is having on his health. We're meeting because he trusts me and he knows that I've been an anxious Christian, so anxious that my health has also been affected by it. I've known all the 'anxiety' verses since I was 16. "Be anxious for nothing, but…." But, to no avail. I was so anxious at one point in my late 30s that it triggered an autoimmune illness and left me bedridden for four months.

This week's verses bring a perspective that was lost on me in my early, anxious, Christian life. In them, we are invited to join Mary and Martha—Martha busy in the kitchen, brooding; her sister, quietly listening at Jesus' feet. Martha, anxious and distracted in her service. Mary, peaceful, listening. What's the difference? Martha is busy doing. Mary is in the *presence*. While the text doesn't directly tell us this, my guess is that in her serving, Martha missed the presence of her Master *and* of her guests. She put on a good program, but didn't really connect with anyone. In contrast, Mary is in the presence of the Master and, I would guess, had a few deep conversations that put her in the presence of others before they all went home that night.

Bedridden by anxiety. Bedridden by trying to be what I "should" be. Bedridden by trying to "do" anxiety Scriptures in the hope of freedom (pray more, be more thankful, let go and let God!).

What I needed was quiet at the Master's feet. Interestingly, when Martha asks Jesus to have Mary come help her, he responds, "You are anxious and troubled by many things, but *only* one thing is necessary. Mary has chosen the good part, which will not be taken away from her." His presence will never be taken away from us. No matter how pressing the needs of the moment.

What if you were to take some time each day this week to be quiet. To sit and be present at the Master's feet. Even if you can only squeeze out two to three minutes, sit quietly with your eyes closed and know deep in your heart that you are absolutely loved by the God of the universe. That you are safe. That there is really only one thing that is necessary…and you are doing it.

Day 5 – A Voice from Bethany

Mary and Martha
Luke 10:38-42
Ken Morgan

Several years ago I was a member of a military reserve unit. Each year we were required to receive training in the proper use of the gas mask. Since we were a non combat unit, and most of us had not fired a military rifle in years, the possibility of going into a hostile environment where lethal gas might be used was the farthest thing from our minds. Those who had been in the same class hearing the same instructions for several years did not hide the fact that they thought the training was redundant, boring and unnecessary.

I remember one year that was uniquely different. It was during the build-up to the first Gulf War. Saddam Hussein had recently used poison gas against the Kurds, and there was some scuttlebutt that we might be deployed to the region. That year EVERYONE paid attention to the demonstration on proper use of the gas mask. Everyone was an attentive listener. Many asked for instructions to be repeated. When the formal demonstration and instruction were completed, many stayed behind to ask additional questions. That year I learned the difference between "distracted hearing" and "attentive listening". I also learned that when I view something as essential to survival, nothing is more important.

It is clear not only in Luke 10:38-42, but also John 11 and 12, that there was a deep and affectionate relationship between Jesus and these two women. Unlike my experience with the gas mask, there was no boredom or disdain, however the distinction between distracted hearing and attentive listening still holds. It is probable that Martha was within earshot and HEARD most if not all of what Jesus was saying, but was distracted both by serving and her irritation with her sister's lack of help. Mary, on the other hand, "sat at the Lord's feet and LISTENED." She was giving her full attention not only to the words being spoken, but more importantly to the Person speaking them. In her focused attention to the Savior, Mary not only profited from His words and His presence, but the very decision to take the time to listen freed her from the anxiety experienced by her sister.

> "You keep him in perfect peace whose mind is stayed on you, because he trusts in you." Isaiah 26:3

Day 6 – Journal

How did you see God at work in you this week?

What did you notice about your "life with God" this week?

What was encouraging?

What was challenging?

How is your desire for Him shifting this week?

What was it like to fast this week?

Small Group Discussion for Week 4 ... Losing Anxiety

Prayer/Reflection
Begin with a few moments of quiet before the Lord

Group leader: read Luke 10:38-42. Followed by some time for quiet reflection ...

Under what circumstances are you like Martha? Are there places in your life where you get distracted?

Now, consider how you are like Mary. What practices deepen your prayerful dependence on God?

Discuss as a group ...

Review
What was the main idea of the teaching this week?

What are the implications?

Why does it matter in your life? (be specific to your life, not people in general)
*   *(allow time/space for all in the group to share)*

Practice
From what did you fast? (use caution - consider Matthew 6:16-18)

How was your experience of the fast?

What have you seen God doing in you through this fast?

Share
What else have you noticed about your life with God in the past days/week?
   (look back at your journal from the previous weeks)

Prayer
How can the group pray for your growth in this part of living a Crucified life?

(pray for one another)

WEEK 5 | LOSING AGENDAS

Now Jesus was praying in a certain place, and when he finished, one of his disciples said to him, "Lord, teach us to pray, as John taught his disciples." And he said to them, "When you pray, say:

"Father, hallowed be your name.
Your kingdom come. Give us each day our daily bread, and forgive us our sins, for we ourselves forgive everyone who is indebted to us. And lead us not into temptation."

Luke 11:1-4

Sermon Notes | Luke 11:1-4

Day 1 – Prayer and Fasting

Weekly Fasting Challenge: *the world and its needs*

Consider the following passage:

> "Then Jesus was led up by the Spirit into the wilderness to be tempted by the devil. And after fasting forty days and forty nights, he was hungry." Matthew 4:1-2

> "Jesus takes for granted that his disciples will observe the pious custom of fasting. Strict exercise of self-control is an essential feature of the Christian's life. Such customs have only one purpose – to make the disciples more ready and cheerful to accomplish what God would have done." Dietrich Bonhoeffer, *The Cost of Discipleship*, p. 188.

Prayer: Father, give me eyes to see the world as you see it. Too often, I merely see things from my perspective and feel a sense of frustration or even hopelessness. May I see this world and your creation as you do!

Plan: *fast from complaining.* There are lots of things that can bring us frustration in this world. However, shift your focus and use those frustrations as a reminder to pray and seek His heart for this world.

What will this look like for you?

Scripture for Prayer/Meditation during fasting:
Luke 11:1-4

Day 2 – A Voice from our Christian Heritage

With Christ in the School of Prayer
Andrew Murray

"Every teacher knows the power of example. He not only tells the child what to do and how to do it, but shows him how it really can be done. In condescension to our weakness, our heavenly Teacher has given us the very words we are to take with us as we draw near to our Father. We have in them a form of prayer in which there breathes the freshness and fullness of the Eternal Life. So simple that the child can lisp it, so divinely rich that it comprehends all that God can give. A form of prayer that becomes the model and inspiration for all other prayer, and yet always draws us back to itself as the deepest utterance of our souls before God."

Take the words of Jesus' prayer in Luke 11:1-4 and re-write them in the space below in your own words:

Day 3 – Reflection Questions

What new insights do you have about Jesus' prayer from Luke 11?

What do you believe God is personally saying to you from these verses?

How might praying according to the pattern of this prayer shape the way you pray?

Have you even prayed with "set prayers"? What are the advantages? What are potential challenges?

Day 4 – A Voice from Bethany

Story of a Friend at Midnight.
Luke 11:5-8
René Fillingame

Ever knocked down a door as a child or an adult? I haven't but my husband James has. That's another story for another time. However, in Luke 11:5-8, Jesus tells the story of a friend who, figuratively speaking, almost knocks a door down for some bread.

There are three friends in the story: Friend A comes for a visit at an inopportune time, Friend B wants to be hospitable and offer food to his guest, and Friend C who is fast asleep and asked to get up and share his bread. This story is sandwiched (pardon the pun) between the Lord's Prayer and Jesus' exhortation to ask, seek and knock so that we may receive and doors may be opened.

Observing the text, it seems that Friend B's motives were good—to provide hospitality and refreshment to his guest regardless of when he showed up on his doorstep. It appears to me that he wanted God's "will to be done on earth as it is in heaven" so he kept knocking and asking Friend C to help him. God, unlike Friend C, "will neither slumber nor sleep" (Psalm 121:4). He is not annoyed by our asking and knocking; rather He encourages it. The bottom line of this story seems to be...persist in prayer!

Author Bob Goff has said, "Maybe there are times when we think a door has been closed and, instead of misinterpreting the circumstances, God wants us to kick it down. Or perhaps just sit outside of it long enough until somebody tells us we can come in."

For over five years I have been persistently asking God to change the financial circumstances of my life. James and I have been working hard to bring change about and we know God is in control of all things (I Timothy 6:15). We also continue to examine our motives as we pray. We trust our good and loving Father and pray for His will to be accomplished in our lives and we know it is...while we wait. He is building our trust in who He is and keeping us dependent on Him.

Ultimately we know that His will for us is to declare who He is during times of struggle and blessing. I continue to knock though, because weddings must be paid for, wisdom teeth need taken out and we won't be young forever.

Have you given up asking God for something that you believe to be His will? Keep asking, seeking, and knocking and sometimes…knock a door down!

Day 5 – A Voice from Bethany

Losing Agendas
Luke 11:11-13
Jim Harte

Our Father…

"What father among you, if his son asks …."

If his son asks? Any father soon learns his child is full of questions. The desire to know about things is a wholesome part of a child's life. And any failure on our part to respond to the question only intensifies the asking. It gets louder and louder. Our silence only animates things.

Surprisingly, this lesson on prayer from Jesus and the following stories brought to mind a question asked of me. One evening several years ago, our son Chuck said, **"Dad, can we talk?"** He was struggling with depression, in his forties and living with us at the time. I had given him a book, along with the Bible, which I suggested would change his life. I assumed he wanted to discuss the book, and had some other questions.

We sat down and I opened my Bible. He immediately slammed it shut in frustration. **"Dad, I want to talk, can't we just talk?"** Obviously, I did not understand his question. I wanted to help, to fix things. If he would only listen, straighten up and make right choices in his life everything would be fine. But, he was listening. What he heard screaming in his heart was, "Something is wrong with me. I am unlovable." He was saying to me, "Dad, I can't do this! If this is what it takes to win your love, there is no hope for me."

What was the question? Good intentions can be disastrous. I had the answers, but to the wrong question. He was asking me to join him in the struggle for his soul, to listen and embrace him in my love. He wanted to believe in his father's love. He wanted to come home. He wanted me. It was a tearful, and painful, and joyous evening.

"…. for a fish, will instead of a fish give him a serpent?"

I would!

The terrible pain shattered all illusions. Our relationship had been broken. We did not know each other. I think we both woke to the reality that God had other plans for our lives. All our expectations were gone. Everything was out in the open. A freedom to be honest was beginning to make its appearance in our struggles.

The diagnosis of a virulent cancer in Chuck quickened the healing process. We were drawn together against a common enemy. We began experiencing together what it meant to let God have His way with us. It was a battle for our hearts. Our love for one another grew in the urgency of the moment. Cancer lost its battle at the Cross of Christ.

Freedom and the experience of the Father's love in Christ are now our comfort. Good gifts.

"…. how much more will the heavenly Father give the Holy Spirit to those who ask Him."

Day 6 – Journal

How did you see God at work in you this week?

What did you notice about your "life with God" this week?

What was encouraging?

What was challenging?

How is your desire for Him shifting this week?

What was it like to fast this week?

Small Group Discussion for Week 5 ... Losing Agendas

Prayer/Reflection
Pray the Lord's Prayer together as a group from Luke 11:1-4.

Group leader: lead the group through a time of reflective prayer based on the Lord's Prayer. Read a part of the prayer out loud and allow the group to quietly reflect and pray on their own, putting that part of the prayer into their own words. After a few moments, go to the next part of the prayer and progress similarly until you reach the end of the prayer.

How does this prayer shape the way we pray?

Review
What was the main idea of the teaching this week?

What are the implications?

Why does it matter in your life? (be specific to your life, not people in general)
(allow time/space for all in the group to share)

Practice
From what did you fast? (use caution - consider Matthew 6:16-18)

How has your experience of the fast been?

What have you seen God doing in you through this fast?

Share
What else have you noticed about your life with God in the past days/week?
(look back at your journal from the previous weeks)

Prayer
How can the group pray for your growth in this part of living a Crucified life?

(pray for one another)

WEEK 6 | LOSING APPEARANCES

While Jesus was speaking, a Pharisee asked him to dine with him, so he went in and reclined at table. The Pharisee was astonished to see that he did not first wash before dinner. And the Lord said to him, "Now you Pharisees cleanse the outside of the cup and of the dish, but inside you are full of greed and wickedness. You fools! Did not he who made the outside make the inside also? But give as alms those things that are within, and behold, everything is clean for you.

"But woe to you Pharisees! For you tithe mint and rue and every herb, and neglect justice and the love of God. These you ought to have done, without neglecting the others. Woe to you Pharisees! For you love the best seat in the synagogues and greetings in the marketplaces. Woe to you! For you are like unmarked graves, and people walk over them without knowing it."

Luke 11:37-44

Sermon Notes | Luke 11:37-52

Day 1 – Prayer and Fasting

Weekly Fasting Challenge: *the church and its leaders*

Consider the following passage:

"Behold, how good and pleasant it is when brothers dwell in unity!" Psalm 133:1

"Fasting, if we conceive of it truly, must not ... be confined to the question of food and drink; fasting should really be made to include abstinence from anything which is legitimate in and of itself for the sake of some special spiritual purpose. There are many bodily functions which are right and normal and perfectly legitimate, but which for special peculiar reasons in certain circumstances should be controlled. That is fasting." Martin Lloyd-Jones. *Studies in the Sermon on the Mount,* p. 38.

Prayer: Father, I know that you desire unity among your people. As a church, may we be honest and work through issues and concerns so that true unity can exist. I let go of clinging to appearances so that I can live in grace *and* truth.

Plan: We often choose to "appear" in ways that are not consistent with the "real us." Choose to fast from an "appearance" this week. You might fast from "referring to yourself in conversation" or perhaps you might choose to do some act of service anonymously. Be creative and prayerful in what you choose.

What will you do?

When will you do it?

Scripture for Prayer/Meditation during fasting:
Psalm 133:1

Day 2 – A Voice from our Christian Heritage
The Moral Temptation
John Coe

The moral temptation is the attempt to deal with our spiritual failure, guilt and shame by means of spiritual efforts, by attempting to perfect oneself in the power of the flesh or the self. It is the attempt of the well-intentioned believer to use spiritual formation, spiritual disciplines, ministry, service, obedience – all good in general - as a way to relieve the burden of spiritual failure, lack of love and the guilt and shame that results. It is the temptation to try to relieve a burden that Christ alone can relieve. To carry such a burden is an awful load to carry.

My thesis or concern is simply this: That no amount of spiritual effort on our part can ever relieve us of our burden of shame and guilt in the Christian life except Christ, that no amount of effort in spiritual formation, in doing spiritual discipline, in ministry can deal with the problems related to sin, shame and guilt. What I have just described is what the secular moralists of all the ages have attempted to do, namely, to use morality as a defense against seeing their need for a savior.

Rather, the Christian life and true spiritual formation denounce the moralistic life as a way to find happiness, to please God, to deal with one's failure and subsequent guilt and shame. Instead, the Christian life is about Christ and less about our efforts. It is about what He has done, and about our life "in Christ," and how to open the heart to this New Covenant life dependent on the Spirit, and how to obey in light of this new life. This is an obedience of abiding in the Vine and open to the Life of God living within. It is an obedience, but not one of moralism. It is more about participation in a new life than imitation of that life.

The truth is that most believers are daily tempted by moralism or "moral formation." Paul the Apostle – one who was deeply acquainted with moralism – knew that the believer would be tempted by this and addressed this problem to the Galatians.

"You foolish Galatians, who has bewitched you, before

whose eyes Jesus Christ was publicly portrayed as crucified? This is the only thing I want to find out from you: did you receive the Spirit by the works of the Law or by hearing with faith? Are you so foolish? Having begun by the Spirit [a relationship by faith] are you now being perfected by the flesh?" (Gal. 3:1-3)

1st Question: How do you know whether you are a Christian moralist? How do you know whether you are susceptible to the moral temptation?

A primary test is to determine whether one is tempted by Christian moralism is as follows. Whenever you are convicted by sin (e.g., from a sermon or the Scriptures) and your first and abiding response in conscience to guilt is "I will do better, I need to work on that," then you know you struggle with being a moralist. Then you know you are trying to use obedience and your own efforts as the primary response to deal with sin, guilt and shame before God. However, this response to sin and conviction is unhealthy and contrary to what is prescribed in the Scriptures. It signals the presence of an unhealthy (neurotic or ill-trained) conscience.

In his letter to the Galatians, Paul tells us that the law of God was a tutor to lead us to Christ, not to morally train the believer.

"But before faith came, we were kept in custody under the law, being shut up to the faith that was later to be revealed. Therefore, the law has become our tutor to lead us to Christ, that we may be justified by faith. But now that faith has come, we are no longer under a tutor." (Gal. 3:23-25)

2nd Question: How can we resist this temptation to be a Christian moralist and learn to depend upon the cross and Spirit?

The remedy to our moralism lies in the Spirit's application of the reality of the gospel to our hearts in daily experience. To put it another way, we resist the temptation of moral formation by opening our heart and mind deeply to the reality of Christ's work on the cross in justification by the Spirit.

Paul the Apostle informs us of our justification in the following words:

"He made Him who knew no sin to be sin on our behalf that we might become the righteousness of God in Him." (2 Cor. 5:21) and " . . . that I may gain Christ, and may be found in him, not having a righteousness of my own derived from the Law, but that which is through faith in Christ, the righteousness that comes from God on the basis of faith . . . ." (Phil. 3:8-9)

Embedded in these two texts is the truth that the Reformers called "double imputation," in which the Father imputes, attributes, or ascribes certain realities to the believer. The two imputations that make up the heart of Christ's work on the cross for us are as follows:

1.   If all your sins are truly imputed to Christ so there is no condemnation, *then come out of hiding in your prayer life and be honest with God.* You have nothing to lose but to open more deeply to your need of Him and the daily forgiveness of the cross.
2.   If Christ's righteousness, not your own, has really been imputed to you so that you are totally accepted by the Father as in the Son, *then stop trying to cover your badness by being good* but in full confession of your badness and failure, obey in *light* of your failure and what He has done for you.

One of the most important spiritual disciplines for daily resisting the temptation of moral formation is to open and center the heart with the Spirit on these two realities of full pardon and full acceptance. Sometimes our moralism has to do with not really accepting the reality of our full pardon from the condemnation of sin. In this case, we seek to hide from our sin by being good, for it is too painful to see our sin as it is insofar as we experience guilt as condemnation. As an antidote to this malady, we must come out of hiding in prayer and open deeply to the truth of our sins and how these have been imputed to Christ, that there is no *condemnation* for those in Christ (Rom. 8:1), so that we may open deeply to the Spirit applying forgiveness and love in our experience.

Day 3 – Reflection Questions

What new insights do you have about Luke 11:37-52?

What do you believe God is personally saying to you from these verses?

How are you seeing God at work in you so far this week?

How is Jesus' view of peace different from the world? Different from yours?

Day 4 – A Voice from Bethany

Authenticity
Michael Donnelly
Luke 11:37-52

Authenticity in the dictionary has one definition: *The quality of being authentic; genuineness.* However, the word *authentic* has several definitions, the first being, *not false or copied; genuine.* When a dictionary definition relies on informing the reader of what something *is not*, there is an implication that the reader understands the meaning of the word from a variety of relational qualities.

In this passage from Luke, the tension between the outside and the inside of the cup holds the relational story of my life's experience. Verses 37-52, positioned in relationship to verse 33, introduce Jesus shining a light on the woes of men.

This Scriptural passage challenges me on a variety of levels. I can be tempted to define myself by what I believe I am *not*. I can be similar to the Pharisees and Lawyers sitting at the table with Jesus when I allow myself to take comfort in the thought that, at least I am not as bad as… and I fill in the blank. Moreover, I can *become* "the blank" by a declaration of what *I am not* because I hide from the relationship to *who I am*. Often I am defined by my work, by my relationships, by that which is measurable and observable – by the "outside of the cup". Though the outside of the cup has value, it is from the inside that I drink. It is with the light of the Lord that I must look inside the cup to who I am.

Jesus brings to light for me an understanding of authenticity through the work of the Holy Spirit. I must look at the cup with earnestness from the inside. I wonder how often I stand at the door with the key in my hand and do not enter into the relationship fully with Jesus. An author once said, "There are some who stand on the rim of the cup and experience the awe of God and there are those that dive into the middle of the cup and learn to swim with God."

To stand in the center of the dry cup is to stand repentant so the Lord can fill the cup with His blessings and I can learn to swim.

Day 5 – A Voice from Bethany

Developing a Heart for God
Luke 11:37-52
Joel Nevius

Our culture is great at marketing. We have an amazing ability to make unattractive things seem better than they actually are. When we see a McDonald's commercial on TV, the cheeseburgers look quality-made: the buns are fluffy, the patty looks thick and juicy, and the lettuce and tomato look like they were picked fresh from a garden. The problem is that neither you, me, or anyone else has ever received a burger like that from McDonald's. The bun is always squished, the patty is thin and sliding out of the bun, the cheese is sticking to the wrapper, and the lettuce and tomatoes are far from fresh. McDonald's is a multi-billion dollar corporation that places a bigger emphasis on advertising a quality product than actually producing a quality product.

In this passage in Luke, we see Jesus harshly rebuking the Pharisees who had perfected the art of advertising a heart of devotion to the God of Israel, rather than actually having one. Their devotion to God seemed pure, innocent, and virtuous on the outside to everyone watching...except Jesus. Jesus points out this blatant hypocrisy: "Now you Pharisees cleanse the outside of the cup and of the dish, but inside you are full of greed and wickedness."

Jesus is calling our attention to a sobering truth: We waste our time with external displays of piety when our hearts aren't motivated by God's heart. God wants the very center of our souls, not simply the periphery that others see. He knows that once He takes care of our hearts, then our behavior will naturally follow. He goes on to say in vv. 40-41: "You fools! Did not he who made the outside make the inside also? But give as alms those things that are within, and behold, everything is clean for you."

Jesus is challenging the Pharisees to stop focusing on the purification of their public personas at the expense of the purification of their souls.

When Jesus has our heart, he has everything. If Jesus has everything but our heart, then we haven't given him anything.

Jesus, crucify my tendency to merely advertise an appearance of devotion to you and others, and replace it with a genuine love and devotion of You. I leave the outward results for your Holy Spirit to manifest in His timing and for Your glory. Amen.

Day 6 – Journal

How did you see God at work in you this week?

What did you notice about your "life with God" this week?

What was encouraging?

What was challenging?

How is your desire for Him shifting this week?

What was it like to fast this week?

Small Group Discussion for Week 6 ... Losing Appearances

Prayer/Reflection
Begin with a few moments of quiet before the Lord

Group leader: slowly read through Luke 11:37-52 followed by silence. Group participants: As you listen prayerfully with eyes closed, notice the word or phrase that stands out to you. In the silence that follows, talk to the Lord about that word or phrase and reflect on why it is important.

Is there anyone in the group that would like to share what stood out to them?

Review
What was the main idea of the teaching this week?

What are the implications?

Why does it matter in your life? (be specific to your life, not people in general)
   (allow time/space for all in the group to share)

Practice
From what did you fast? (use caution - consider Matthew 6:16-18)

How was your experience of the fast?

What have you seen God doing in you through this fast?

Share
What else have you noticed about your life with God in the past days/week?
   (look back at your journal from the previous weeks)

Prayer
How can the group pray for your growth in this part of living a Crucified life?

(pray for one another)

WEEK 7 | LOSING ALLEGIANCES

"I came to cast fire on the earth, and would that it were already kindled! I have a baptism to be baptized with, and how great is my distress until it is accomplished! Do you think that I have come to give peace on earth? No, I tell you, but rather division. For from now on in one house there will be five divided, three against two and two against three. They will be divided, father against son and son against father, mother against daughter and daughter against mother, mother-in-law against her daughter-in-law and daughter-in-law against mother-in-law."

Luke 12:49-53

Sermon Notes | Luke 12:49-53

Day 1 – Prayer and Fasting

Weekly Fasting Challenge: *in order to give*

Consider the following passage:

"For you know the grace of our Lord Jesus Christ, that though he was rich, yet for your sake he became poor, so that you by his poverty might become rich." 2 Corinthians 8:9

"Self-indulgence is the enemy of gratitude, and self-discipline usually its friend and generator. That is why gluttony is a deadly sin. The early desert fathers believed that a person's appetites are linked: full stomachs and jaded palates take the edge away from our hunger and thirst for righteousness. They spoil the appetite for God." Cornelius Plantinga, quoted by Donald Whitney in *Spiritual Disciplines for the Christian Life*, p. 151.

Prayer: Ask God to show you an area of your life where you can go "without" in order to help someone in need.

Plan: What can you go without this week?

What will you do?

To whom will you give? (make it anonymous to honor Jesus' words in Mt 6:1)

Scripture for Prayer/Meditation during fasting:
2 Corinthians 8:9

CRUCIFIED

Day 2 – A Voice from our Christian Heritage

People Pleasing is Idolatry
Rick Warren

"I'm not trying to win the approval of people, but of God. If pleasing people were my goal, I would not be Christ's servant." (Galatians 1:10 NLT)

In life, you only have to please one person. And that is your Creator. You only have to please the Lord, the one who made you and has a purpose for your life.

That simplifies life enormously! You only need one person's approval: God's.

Jesus said it like this in John 5:30: *"I don't try to please myself, but I try to please the One who sent me"* (NCV). He said, "I'm living for an audience of one."

You may have never realized this, but people-pleasing is a form of idolatry. The first commandment in the Ten Commandments is, "Don't have any gods before me." Anything you put before God becomes a god. So a boat could be a god. A career could be a god. A girlfriend could be a god. Golf could be a god. Anything that becomes number one in your life that isn't God becomes your god.

The second commandment is, "Don't make any idols." Anything that replaces God in your life is an idol. Success can be an idol. Money can be an idol. Sex can be an idol. A relationship can become an idol. If that relationship to your girlfriend, your wife, your boss, or your friend is more important than God, it's an idol.

When you are a people-pleaser, you have allowed something other than God to take first place. All of a sudden it becomes god in your life, because you are allowing the opinion of others to matter more than God's opinion. What they think of you matters more than what God thinks of you. You don't want to tell them you're a Christian because they might think less of you. For example, you don't want them to know you go to church because they may not like you. At that point, you have another god in your life. You have an idol.

88

You only have to please one person. Paul says in Galatians 1:10, *"I'm not trying to win the approval of people, but of God. If pleasing people were my goal, I would not be Christ's servant"* (NLT).

Day 3 – Reflection Questions

What new insights do you have about Luke 12:49-53?

What do you believe God is personally saying to you from these verses?

How are you seeing God at work in you so far this week?

When do you see people-pleasing affect you?

What would it mean for you to let go of people-pleasing?

Day 4 – A Voice from Bethany

Love Without Demands
1 John 4:18a & 19
Michael and Rebekah Stines

Experiencing true, agape love has been such a significant reality in our lives that it has caused us both to love deeper, truer and to let go of fear in many ways. We know that fear in our hearts is what causes us to make demands of God. An insecurity or a need for security causes us to hold onto things that God may want us to let go of. In subtle ways, but never directly spoken or specifically thought, we demand things from God related to our wellbeing as we see it.

We've faced many challenges in the past four years. One of them was an unexpected career change for me, Michael. I abruptly went from making a middle class income to being unemployed and having a hard time finding a "good" job. It was scary! We had grown accustomed to living a certain way and, even though I never would have said it, I expected that we would continue to live that way. I had these unspoken demands of God based on what I wanted or felt like we "needed", not just in relation to my salary, but possessions and relationships as well. When I was looking for new jobs, I expected Him to come through and land me a great paying job. After a couple months of being unemployed, I eventually settled for a job that resulted in an almost 70% cut in my salary. We had to let go of all expectations and demands we were placing on God, and just rely on Him and wait.

Honestly, I don't think I did a very good job of that at first. My fears ruled me instead of God's love and my love for Him. As we were living "without" so much, God provided what we needed as He promises in Luke 12:22-32 and Matthew 6:25-34 (among other places). It wasn't until almost two years later that God provided a job that moved us back above the poverty line. However, during those two years, we learned in a whole new way how to love without demands but with bold reliance upon God and His sovereignty.

Are you aware of any demands you make of God either knowingly or unknowingly? We encourage you to take some time to sit in His presence and invite Him to show you what they are.

Do you trust that God knows what you need? If so, are you ready to release those demands that you make of Him?

What obstacles might prevent you from fully releasing those areas to the Lord?

Meditate on what your life would look like if you loved without demands – the way you love, the way you trust, and the way you experience His presence.

Day 5 – A Voice from Bethany

Love that is Pure
Luke 12:49-53
Doug Kelley

Jesus' words are shocking: "Do you suppose that I came to grant peace on earth? I tell you, no, but rather division." Didn't Jesus come to bring peace? The short answer is, "Yes," of course Jesus came to bring peace. But, that said, think of what this peace cost him—his broken body hanging on the cross. Jesus' perfect love for us caused division. Fear resulted in violence as people clung to allegiances and a worldview that helped them feel safe, in control and at peace.

Maintaining differences is one of the ways people seek personal peace. There is great security in a black and white worldview. A simple Yes to this and No to that keeps one's world predictable and sure. Yet, Jesus tells us the peace He is giving is not what the world gives: "My peace I give to you; not as the world gives do I give to you. Do not let your heart be troubled, nor let it be fearful" (John 14:27).

The peace the world gives comes from division. If I can align myself with the right groups, right thinking, right behavior then I have some predictability and control over my world. Yet, as Dr. Phil says, "How's that working for ya?" This is a false peace because we spend our entire lives trying to maintain the distinctions that keep our lives predictable—even when it means dividing families, communities, or even the Church itself, in order to keep our worldview intact.

Jesus came to blow apart this worldview. Jesus came teaching that pure love is a way of seeing, a way of knowing. That "perfect love casts out all fear," and, so, destroys our need for all false allegiance. As the Apostle Paul puts it, "There is no longer Jew or Gentile, slave or free, male or female. For you are all one in Christ Jesus" (Gal 3:28).

If you choose to love as Jesus did, you too will create division. People will be unsettled by your lack of allegiance to certain ideas, groups, or issues. They will be disturbed by your love for others and peace in Him.

Think of a false allegiance, an idea you've been clinging to because it helps you feel 'safe' by keeping your worldview intact (we all have them)—Muslims are.... Undocumented persons should.... Women are.... Democrats think.... Africa is.... Good Christians do.... What if you gave up one false allegiance for a week? What if this week you chose to find peace in His perfect love and freely offer that love to others?

Day 6 – Journal

How did you see God at work in you this week?

What did you notice about your "life with God" this week?

What was encouraging?

What was challenging?

How is your desire for Him shifting this week?

What was it like to fast this week?

Small Group Discussion for Week 7 ... Losing Allegiances

Prayer/Reflection
Begin with a few moments of quiet before the Lord

Group leader: read through Luke 12:49-53. Allow the group to quietly listen followed by a time of personal reflection.

> *What relationships do you need to entrust to the Lord?*

> *Are there places in your life where you struggle with people-pleasing? Why or why not?*

Share your reflections as a group ...

Review
What was the main idea of the teaching this week?

What are the implications?

Why does it matter in your life? (be specific to your life, not people in general) (allow time/space for all in the group to share)

Practice
From what did you fast? (use caution - consider Matthew 6:16-18)

How was your experience of the fast?

What have you seen God doing in you through this fast?

Share

What else have you noticed about your life with God in the past days/week? (look back at your journal from the previous weeks)

Prayer

How can the group pray for your growth in this part of living a Crucified life?

(pray for one another)

WEEK 8 | FINDING ACCEPTANCE

"But when he came to himself, he said, 'How many of my father's hired servants have more than enough bread, but I perish here with hunger! I will arise and go to my father, and I will say to him, "Father, I have sinned against heaven and before you. I am no longer worthy to be called your son. Treat me as one of your hired servants."' And he arose and came to his father. But while he was still a long way off, his father saw him and felt compassion, and ran and embraced him and kissed him. And the son said to him, 'Father, I have sinned against heaven and before you. I am no longer worthy to be called your son.' But the father said to his servants, 'Bring quickly the best robe, and put it on him, and put a ring on his hand, and shoes on his feet. And bring the fattened calf and kill it, and let us eat and celebrate. For this my son was dead, and is alive again; he was lost, and is found.' And they began to celebrate.

Luke 15:17-24

Sermon Notes | Luke 15:11-32

Day 1 – Prayer and Fasting

Weekly Fasting Challenge: *celebration*
This week is a week of celebration. No fasting, simply celebrating the resurrection.

Consider the following passage:

"For everything created by God is good, and nothing is to be rejected if it is received with thanksgiving, for it is made holy by the word of God and prayer." 1 Timothy 4:4-5

Prayer: *Father, thank you for giving me life in Christ. Thank you that I can enjoy all things because you are the giver of all good gifts.*

Plan: What is an activity that you enjoy? Set aside time to enjoy that activity by looking at it through the lens of the word of God and prayer.

What will you do?

When will you do it?

Scripture for Prayer/Meditation during fasting:
James 1:17

Day 2 – A Voice from our Christian Heritage

"The exact and discriminate meaning of the word *grace* should be crystal clear to every child of God. With such insight only can he feed his own soul on the inexhaustible riches which it unfolds, and with such understanding only can he be enabled clearly to pass on to others its marvelous, transforming theme. *Grace* means pure unrecompensed kindness and favor.

"Grace is neither treating a person as he deserves, nor treating a person better than he deserves. It is treating a person graciously without the slightest reference to what he deserves. Grace is infinite love expressing itself in infinite goodness."

Lewis Sperry Chafer, *Grace*

"Let's imagine that you have a six-year-old son whom you love dearly. Tragically, one day you discover that your son was horribly murdered. After a lengthy search, the investigators find the killer. You have a choice. If you used every means in your power to kill the murderer for his crime, that would be vengeance. If, however, you are content to sit back and let the legal authorities take over and execute on him what is proper – a fair trial, a plea of guilty, capital punishment – that is justice. But if you should plead for the pardon of the murderer, forgive him completely, invite him into your home, and adopt him as your own son, that is grace."

Chuck Swindoll, *Grace Awakening*

We enjoy His grace in our lives to the extent that we've "let go" of our reliance on other things: ambition, attachments, anxiety, agendas, appearances, and allegiances. As we let go (like the prodigal son), we come home. We allow Him to love us.

In the space below, write out a prayer to God the Father. Tell Him what you are leaving behind. Thank Him for grace. Ask Him if there is something that He desires to tell you about your life in Him.

(remember: this "leaving behind" is the essence of the crucified life and it is a daily exercise!)

Day 3 – Reflection Questions

What new insights do you have about Luke 15?

What do you believe God is personally saying to you from these verses?

How are you seeing God at work in you so far this week?

Why is grace so significant? How does it change the way you approach all of life?

Day 4 – A Voice from Bethany

God's Celebration of Us
Luke 15
Ken Morgan

Recently, I was a guest at a cabin in northern Arizona. One morning in the course of taking a walk, I passed by a very large and luxurious cabin. It had recently caught fire and burned; it was a total loss.

I was told that a grandfather had granted permission to his grandson to use the cabin. An out of control party by the grandson and his friends led to the total destruction of a very expensive mountain retreat.

As we walked by, I wondered what went through the grandson's mind as he saw the fire rage out of control. What did he say to his grandfather when he broke the news? How did his grandfather respond? What about the other family members who saw a significant share of the family inheritance go up in smoke, to say nothing of the missed family events resulting from the carelessness of one family member. Would the grandson ever feel welcome at future family events? Would this loss lead to endless divisive family discussions?

Luke 15 tells of a similar dynamic when a foolish son wastes 1/3 of his father's net worth in a series of careless and selfish decisions. In the story of the lost son, the focus of the father was not on the loss of property or personal prestige brought on by the son's foolish choices. His only concern was the reconciliation of his family.

When the wayward son returned in humiliation, the father chose not to act like a vengeful father, he did not even act like the distinguished gentleman that he was. He behaved like a giddy child, overcome with joy and delight at the return of his son. His only sadness was the refusal of the older brother to share his joy.

In this beautiful picture we see the heart of our Heavenly Father. He delights when the wayward and rebellious turn to Him. His only sadness comes from seeing the reluctance or refusal of other family members to enter into His joy and happiness.

"We speak for Christ when we plead, 'Come back to God!' For God made Christ, who never sinned, to be the offering for our sin, so that we could be made right with God through Christ." (2 Cor 5:20-21 – NLT)

Day 5 – A Voice from Bethany

Finding Rest
Luke 15
Ted Wueste

In Matthew 11:28-30, Jesus invites us into His way of living. He boldly proclaims that as we adopt the "unforced rhythms of grace" (MSG), we will be at rest. There is a way of doing life that appears to give life, but it actually leaves us tired.

The story that Jesus tells about a father and son in Luke 15 is a picture of this kind of rest. The rest that is described is the rest that can come when we live with grace as our bottom line. We often think of grace as being about forgiveness. It is that, but it is so much more. Grace is God's unmerited favor toward those who are in Christ. It means forgiveness from sin, but it also means that He is "for us". He celebrates us and cheers for us and gives to us. We see this in the story of the father and son. Not only did the father forgive (he didn't even listen to the son's whole confession) but he gave him a robe and a ring and a party. He celebrated him.

How amazing to think that God the Father celebrates us! How incredible to realize that He is for us! He doesn't sit back and wait but He is constantly running to us. He is involved in our lives moment to moment. We don't have to ask Him to "show up". He is already graciously present. He gives, He serves and He sacrifices for us.

How humbling to consider that the God who deserves all of our worship acts this way toward us. It is reminiscent of Jesus washing the disciples' feet. How do we respond when we begin to understand His gracious ways? Jesus suggests in Matthew 11 that there is a rhythm to living by grace. What are those rhythms?

Grace means that I don't have to prove myself or my worthiness.
Grace means that He is already present and at work in my life.
Grace means that I am loved right where I am … the good, the bad, and the ugly.
Grace means that He is cheering for me right now.
Grace means that He will give me whatever I need to be everything He made me to be.

How do you need to begin living according to these realities? As you do, you will begin to live according to the rhythms of grace!

PRAYER: Father, I want to see life through the lens of Your grace. Help me to remember Your grace that is at work in me today. May I live in response to the truth of Your grace. Amen.

Day 6 – Journal

How did you see God at work in you this week?

What did you notice about your "life with God" this week?

What was encouraging?

What was challenging?

How is your desire for Him shifting this week?

Small Group Discussion for Week 8 ... Finding Acceptance

Prayer/Reflection
Begin with a time of prayerful worship.

Group leader: read Psalm 100 followed by a time of prayerful reflection ...

How have you seen God at work in you over these last eight weeks?

Is there anyone in the group that would like to share what stood out to them?

Review
What was the main idea of the teaching this week?

What are the implications?

Why does it matter in your life? (be specific to your life, not people in general)
(allow time/space for all in the group to share)

Practice
What will you take with you from this study?

How will you continue to utilize fasting as a tool for further growth in your relationship with God?

Prayer
How can the group pray for your growth in this part of living a Crucified life?

(pray for one another)

Notes

FASTING | ENRICHMENT CLASS NOTES

Then the disciples of John came to him, saying, "Why do we and the Pharisees fast, but your disciples do not fast?" And Jesus said to them, "Can the wedding guests mourn as long as the bridegroom is with them? The days will come when the bridegroom is taken away from them, and then they will fast.

Matthew 9:14-15

Notes | Week 1

Notes | Week 2

Notes | Week 3

Notes | Week 4

Notes | Week 5

Notes | Week 6

Notes | Week 7

Notes | Week 8

NEXT STEPS | MY CRUCIFIED PLAN

And he said to them, "Is a lamp brought in to be put under a basket, or under a bed, and not on a stand? For nothing is hidden except to be made manifest; nor is anything secret except to come to light. If anyone has ears to hear, let him hear." And he said to them, "Pay attention to what you hear: with the measure you use, it will be measured to you, and still more will be added to you. For to the one who has, more will be given, and from the one who has not, even what he has will be taken away."

Mark 4:21-25

What will next steps look like for you?

Spend some time in prayer, asking the Father about next steps in your journey with Him.

What things do you need to continue to leave behind?

What practices of fasting will you continue to utilize for the sake of your life with God?

What daily prayer practices will nurture the Crucified Life in you?

With whom will you share the journey? (small group? etc?)

ADDITIONAL NOTES

CRUCIFIED

Finding through Losing

CRUCIFIED